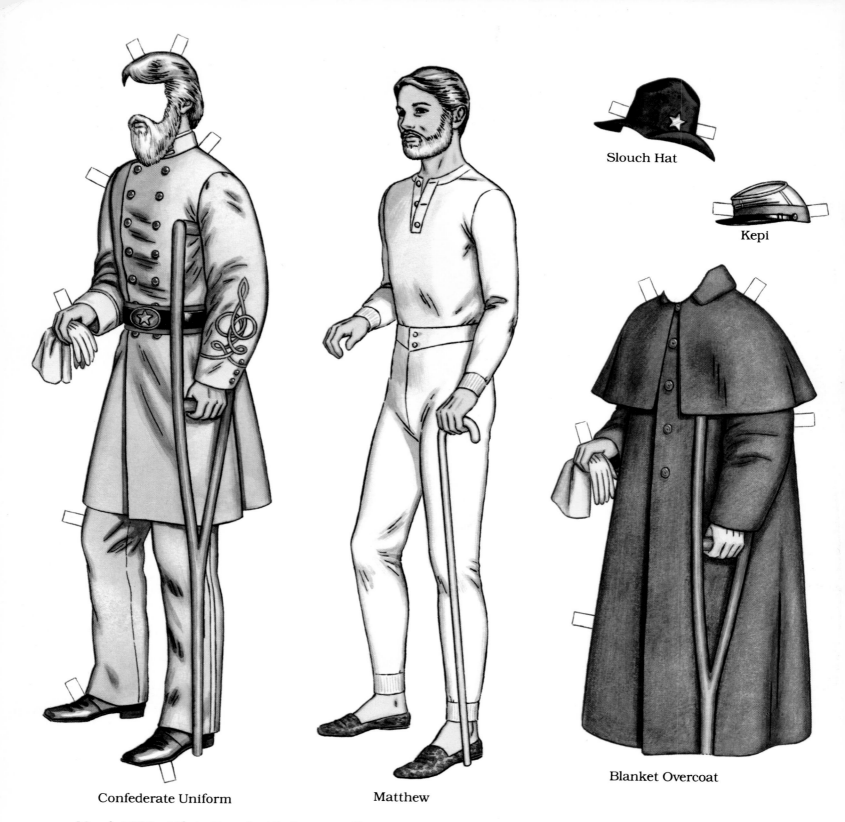

Slouch Hat

Kepi

Confederate Uniform

Matthew

Blanket Overcoat

March 1862—Life is dismal with the men off to war. Made up my mind that we must keep up or go under, though, so I've been knitting for the soldiers—socks and scarves. No money for any piece-goods.

December 1862—Just finished the overcoat for Matthew out of the heavy gray-blue blanket that I had been saving. He is to be furloughed soon. The material was so thick I have pricked my fingers badly trying to make strong back-stitches. All in all, it does look rather nice—and will be warm. The boys made him some carpet slippers to wear around the house—a bit crude, but it's the thought that counts.

January 1863—Matthew has come and gone again. I felt a proper pride to see him looking so fine in his Confederate uniform. A cadet gray frock coat and trousers, gold lieutenant's bars on the collar with a stripe of blue down the side of the trousers and gold braid on the sleeves, a red sash, a black felt slouch hat with a lone star pinned on one side, and a little billed cap of blue (lieutenant's color). He said it is copied from the French Kepi. I think he must wear the little one when he is in battle.

My spirits were rather low, watching him leave, but he said he had to see this terrible thing through. So many have been killed, and the Battle of Fredericksburg left Matthew wounded a year ago. He was still walking with a crutch.

Wild Roses and Calico Bush

Amanda in Chemise, Drawers, and Corset

Chenille Net Snood

Sunbonnet

Dress of Ticking

Outdoor Working Garb

June 1863—Found some wild roses out in the pasture. Transplanted several to the front of the cabin. They should be pretty again by next year. Also moved some calico bushes.

June 1864—All our old working clothes are getting so shabby. I've patched my faded brown broadcloth skirt one more time. Took some sturdy flour sacks and dyed them with pokeberry for a bonnet and apron, but they came out a rather faded red. Made a bodice out of the checked gingham that covered the feather mattress ticking.

August 1864—We are trying to put up all the fruit we can for winter months. Dried bushels of apples and peaches. Did the churning and baking, washing and ironing. Very tired.

April 1865—Received word that Lee's Army has surrendered in Virginia. Matthew likely will be home before too long.

May 1865—I had wanted a new dress for Matthew's homecoming, but calico is too costly—$4-$5 per yard—when you can find it. So made a little frock out of striped ticking and trimmed it with gourd seeds dyed red with cochineal and added black ribbon zigzag bands. Then I knotted a chenille net snood to wear on my chignon. It does look fashionable.

June 1865—I feel thankful that Matthew's duty to his country has been met. He is now home . . . hardly recognized him—he has lost so much weight and has so many scars of the fighting. Sometimes his leg bothers him, and he uses his cane.

"Stack Cake"

Tintype

Silk Dress with Floss Fringe

Mother-of-the-bride Dress

July 1866—Things seem back to normal, sort of. Matthew made a trip to Austin to see about a land grant and brought back some pretty blue plaid silk from the mercantile. I'll have my first fine new dress since the war. How grand I will feel. We've had to "make-do" for so long. Jennie helped me run some dried grape vines in a tuck on my petticoat and turned it into a fair-sized hooped petticoat.

August 1866—Got my new dress made up just in time. An itinerant photographer came by and did a tintype of me and of Matthew. Never had a picture made before.

September 1868—It seems such a short time ago that my daughter, Jennie, was hanging onto my skirts. Now she'll be wearing them. She and James have set the date of their union, and she wants to wear my wedding dress. It's a bit out of style but does fit her perfectly.

October 1868—It never rains but what it pours! John Nathan and Polly Dorsey have decided to make it a double wedding. I will be so busy. Jennie will need some new things and I want to help Polly with her wedding gown since the poor girl doesn't have a mother. My new dress will be ecru buff brilliantine, trimmed with slate satin-bound scallops—the latest thing in trims. I'll order ready-made hooped petticoats from Houston for all three of us; so much nicer than having to wear 4 or 5 regular petticoats as before.

December 1868—Another Christmas wedding—or weddings. Jennie and Polly were both beautiful brides. We had the "Stack Cakes" for each bride. Most of the guests brought a cake layer which we stacked with chunky applesauce made from dried apples, and topped with whipped cream and nuts. Must have been 10 cakes with half a dozen layers in each cake. Shows how popular the girls are. Plenty of cake for more than 75 guests that came from far and near. The dancing afterwards was lively with music from fiddles, accordion, guitars, and harmonica.

Printed Broadcloth Polonaise

"Common Sense" Machine

Horsehair-crinoline

Striped Lawn with Looped Overskirt

March 1870—Matthew has received a land grant for services rendered to the Republic and we will soon be moving onto ranchland near Ft. Griffin. It's just over 100 miles from Dallas, which is a pretty nice development, I hear. Jeremiah will be Matthew's right-hand man.

April 1870—Our circle of love has been completed now with the birth of our first grandchild, Mary Megan—born to Jennie and James Maxwell, in Burnet County, Texas. They named her Megan because it means strong, they said. They have a place up the river a piece and I went over and stayed till we got the baby baptized in the christening dress I made for John Nathan 24 years ago. I'll find it hard to leave the new baby when we move.

June 1870—Well, here we are—living in a tent on the wild, uncultivated rangeland till the house is finished. You can see so far over the rise. Not as many trees as before. No neighbors nearer than 30 miles again, but the fort is only 23 miles away, and we are not too far from the Clear Fork of the Brazos River. Still, I seem to be happy in this scene of life to which I have been introduced.

March 1871—At last, my wish has been fulfilled. I have a new sewing machine. It's a "Common Sense" Machine that Matthew ordered. So remarkable, how it makes real stitches, as good as a tailor could. My first thing to make was a gold print broadcloth with a polonaise draped up in the back over my horsehair-crinoline (or dress improver, as some call it). It looks a little like a cage. I also made a new peach-colored chambray bonnet. Stitched the brim in fancy diamonds. Several neighbor ladies rode all the way over to see how the machine works.

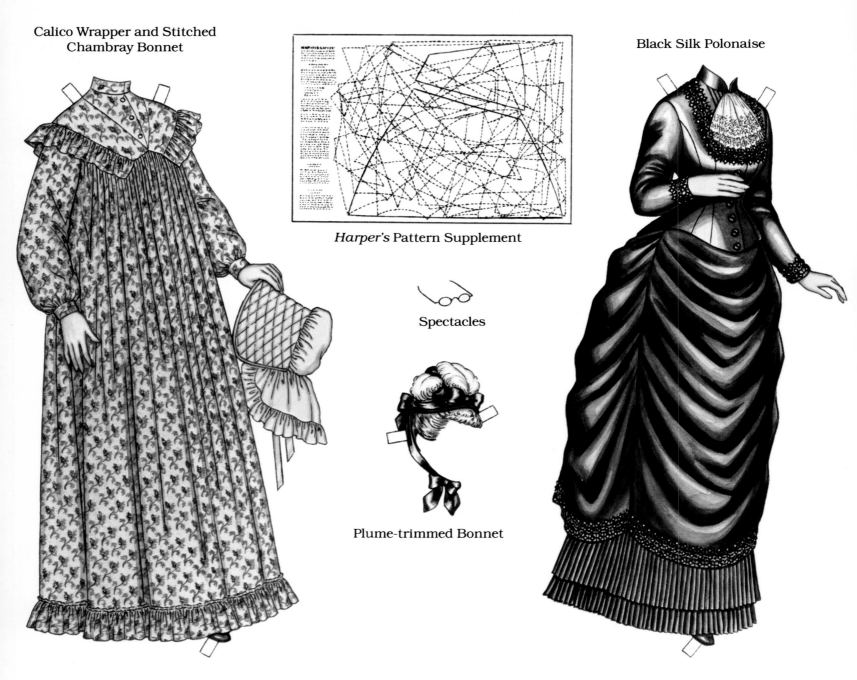

Calico Wrapper and Stitched Chambray Bonnet

Harper's Pattern Supplement

Spectacles

Plume-trimmed Bonnet

Black Silk Polonaise

May 1872—I have my own subscription to *Harper's Bazar* and *Peterson's* now, so I can see what is really fashionable. Little diagrams show the pattern shapes to be traced, and then I enlarge them.

July 1873—Finished my new solferino pink and white striped lawn just in time for wearing to the 4th of July picnic at the fort. It took over 14 yards of material, as I trimmed it with ruffles. The ladies at the fort do dress prettily, but my dress was every bit as nice as the ones they had ordered from B. Altman's in New York, at least Matthew said it was.

January 1874—Jeremiah just learned that the Southwestern University has opened down state in Georgetown last year. He says he will save his money from working the cattle and go there to study law. He reads everything he can get his hands on.

February 1874—Have to help roundup the cattle sometimes, so I generally wear my bonnet and wrappers, but they get caught in the brambles. Just got a big tear in my new calico. Need to make a heavier outfit. It's strange to look out and see the long-horned cattle grazing in the pastures.

April 1874—Sewing is so much faster and easier with my sewing machine. Now *Harper's* has real pattern supplements. Simply trace the pattern shape following the .—.—.—. or ****** etc. Then make the pattern fit the body and then cut out the goods. I have my next outfit planned.

August 1874—Matthew went to Ft. Worth to get some building materials and brought back some goods for me a new black silk dress and dark loden green wool to make a riding suit. Everyone goes on lobo hunts and buffalo hunts, and I might go on the next one.

September 1874—Lots of canning to do and drying the meat and fruit to feed the ranch hands this winter. Need lots of aprons and working clothes. Don't see other women very often.

"Feathered Star and Blazing Sun" Quilt Blocks

Flower-trimmed
Dressy Hat

Heavy Wool Riding Suit and Riding Hat

Velvet-trimmed Linen Princess Sheath

November 1874—I finally got some reading glasses! Have needed them for a long time for all the close work I do. I found an advertisement in the *Harper's* and ordered them. Makes me really look like a grandmother now.

January 1875—Since the blizzard hit, we have to stay inside so much I've been able to work on my new black silk. The eye glasses help! Used a *Harper's* pattern. Such a complicated polonaise. It is three pieced—the bodice, skirt, and a separate, looped-up overskirt, but there is enough goods in it so I can alter it in a few years. A good black silk is so appropriate for a woman my age. I beaded it with jet black beads.

August 1875—Just finished piecing the last block of my "Feathered Star and Blazing Sun," made from Grandmama's old quilt pattern. When I get the blocks together I'll invite the neighbor ladies over.

October 1875—Finished my Paisley-striped heavy linen—the new princess sheath style—just in time for my "spend the day" and quilting party. Ladies from all the surrounding ranches came. What pleasure we had with all the quilting, exchanging recipes and such. Later the men joined us for a barbeque dinner followed by dancing till almost daybreak.

November 1875—I got my riding suit made. Used leather straps and buckles to fasten the basque. I had ordered a riding hat, but I have a feeling I'll wear my bonnet most of the time.

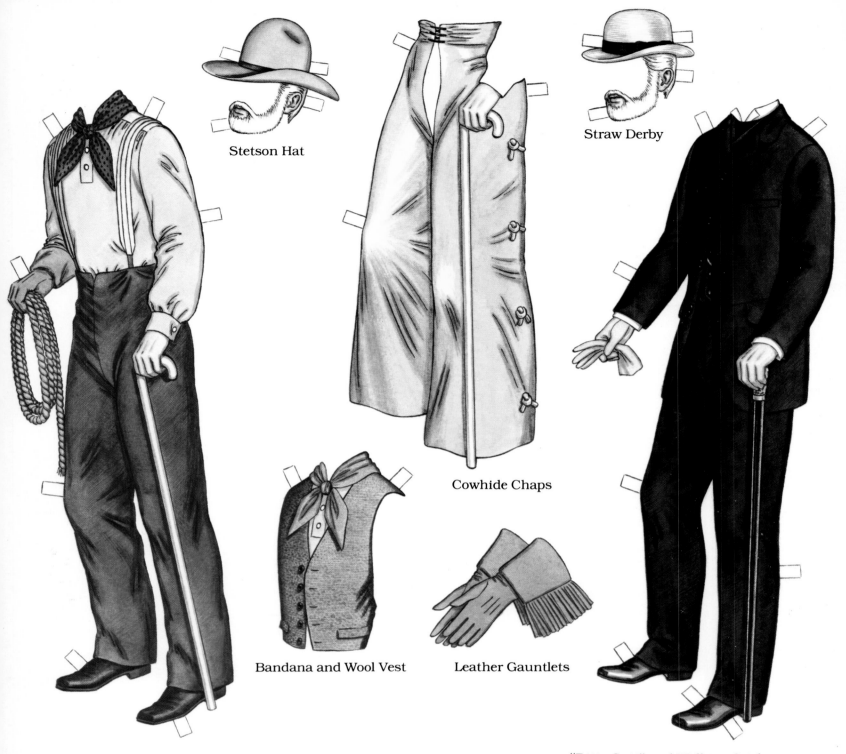

Stetson Hat

Straw Derby

Cowhide Chaps

Bandana and Wool Vest

Leather Gauntlets

Levis and Chambray Shirt

"Ditto Suit" and Walking Stick

December 1875—Matthew is looking more like a cowboy everyday. He just got his first pair of levis—heavy cotton twilled stuff in brown with copper rivets, also cowhide chaps that tie around the legs for protection from the brambles. I made him a striped gingham shirt and he bought a ready-made one of blue chambray at the sutler's. He is never without a vest, his wide-brimmed hat, bandana, and of course his boots. You would never guess that his leg was so bad, except in bad weather he walks with a limp and sometimes uses his cane.

February 1876—The big news is we are going to the Philadelphia Centennial Exposition. Matthew says we will take the Houston and Texas Central train from Dallas to Denison. There in Indian Territory we get on the KATY to St. Louis. The rest of the trip should be easy. Guess it will cost a lot, but Matthew says it's a once in a lifetime opportunity.

Leather Pocketbook

Hand-painted Souvenir Fan

High-top shoes

Silk Taffeta Dress

Velvet-trimmed Traveling Dress

May 1876—Am busy getting things ready for the trip. The Paisley-striped linen dress should be nice to take; also my new black silk. I've cut out a practical rust sateen walking dress that I'll trim with black ciselé velvet. Also have the goods for a Wedgewood blue silk taffeta for dressing up. Matthew ordered valises from Ft. Worth.

August 1876—It was a tedious trip—part by stagecoach and part by rail. Once in the city we stayed in a real hotel. Such wondrous things we saw—moving, working models of all kinds of machines, a telephone you can talk to and sounds go over a wire. Reapers and printing presses and things from all over the world. We walked till I almost dropped trying to see the 167 buildings of wonders. Made a collection of postcards to bring back for everyone to see. Among our souvenirs were hand-painted fans for the girls and fine leather gauntlets for the boys and the ranch hands. Bought new shoes and bonnets at Wanamakers—a beautiful store. Also got Matthew a "ditto suit." It has trousers, vest, and coat to match. Went to the John B. Stetson Co. and bought Matthew's new hat.

Took a short trip to Chester County outside Philadelphia and visited some of Matthew's kinfolks that he hadn't seen for 35 years—since he moved to Texas.

Bombazine Christmas Dress

Cornucopia

Fringe-trimmed Dolman

Cut-velvet Visiting Toilette

April 1880—Seems we are going to build a new house. Cattle prices were good this year and Matthew has plans for an 8-room stone house. He said we will go to Ft. Worth to buy the furniture. Also, there is a dressmaker there who takes your measurements and makes real stylish clothes. They say she charges as much as $15 but will do a less fancy one for $5. I'll order a new black dolman with black serpentine braid and fringe and a red bombazine dress. It's to be made up in the new slim cuirasse-style and should look dignified!

November 1880—The new house was finished in time to have a real Christmas party. All the hands and some of the folks from the fort and nearby ranches will be here. I have lots of baking to do. Good thing I ordered the new red dress while I was in the city. It'll be a right smart Christmas dress.

December 1880—Trimmed the house with evergreen and bows and had the hands bring in a cedar tree that we decorated with stars and lighted candles and fruit. Arranged fruit and nuts in the big cornucopia that I brought back from Philadelphia. We were able to get some oranges and a pineapple freighted in from San Antonio. Ordered favors from *Montgomery Ward Catalogue*—fascinators and clouds for the women and watch fobs for the men.

June 1884—Jennie and James and the children have moved up here into our old house. With their 3 boys, Paul (12), Eric (10), and Stuart, who is only 9 but loves horses, along with John Nathan and John Jr., who is 13, Matthew says he has a substantial backing for working our rangeland. Even with our eight regular hands, it takes all of us working at branding time.

September 1886—Big cattle drive. Other ranchers joined with Matthew and they're herding the cattle to Kansas City to market.

Silk Ottoman

Velvet Bonnet

Made-over Black Silk Dress

Lace-trimmed Challis Tea Gown

December 1886—Couldn't believe my eyes when I saw the pretty dark amber cut-velvet dress Matthew brought me from Kansas City. He had Madame Brown make it up especially for me and said it is called a Visiting Toilette, but I'll wear it for "Sunday Best." It has an elaborate side-draped polonaise and is trimmed with chenille, moire taffeta, bows, and fancy embossed buttons—almost too elegant for my needs, but I admire having it. All the ladies will be so envious.

December 1887—Spent a lot of time this past year making Log Cabin quilts for each of our 7 grandchildren. Don't see them often. Too bad they are growing up so fast. Reworked my ten-year-old black silk dress by slimming down the skirt and getting rid of the polonaise. Added a tucked ivory satin vestfront and some pretty leaf-shaped appliques, and then lined the high-standing fan collar with ivory satin. No one would ever guess it's made over. No wonder a good black silk is so useful. Matthew surprised me with a rose gold locket and new earrings. He still treats me like his bride.

October 1888—The Masonic lodges had a big reunion in the Masonic Hall in Weatherford last week. It was grand to meet so many new people, and Matthew got his 32nd Degree bestowed on him. I wore the new amber velvet dress Matthew brought from Kansas City and had a new gray ottoman I had made for the occasion, using one of the McCall's patterns that I ordered for 35 cents from the *McCall's Bazar Pattern Catalogue*. My gray velvet bonnet was ordered from Marshall Field in Chicago.

April 1889—Used one of my wrapper patterns as a guide in cutting my Nile green challis tea gown, and then added black lace panels over ivory silk satin, black ribbons, and taffeta accents. It's dressy for wearing around the house when company comes.

Postcard Album

Christmas Angel

Greeting Card

Ice Wool Cloud (Shawl)

Silk Taffeta Birthday Dress

Bengaline Reception Dress

August 1889—Since I haven't had a new dress for several years, I ordered some mauvette silk taffeta from *Montgomery Ward & Co.* and combined 2 of my *McCall's* patterns. It is rather chic, if I do say so myself. I especially like the sleeves. They are very different with the high puff and shoulder cap.

September 1889—Was I surprised when the children and grandchildren all showed up for my 65th birthday. They brought cakes and pies and roasted chickens, hams, and barbeque—what a feast! Many of the neighbors and friends came. Wore my new silk. Jeremiah, who is now an attorney in Austin, rode the train up to Ft. Worth, and then came on by stagecoach. He brought me a dandy postcard album. Matthew's gift was a pretty sparkling angel to top the Christmas tree. I was filled with unspeakable joy.

November 1890—All the family will be together this year for Christmas—the first time in many years. For the first time we have gotten Christmas greeting cards to mail to our family and friends. There's to be another wedding. I am finishing the wedding dress for our eldest granddaughter, Mary Megan. She is almost my size and looks like I did at 20, but with lighter hair.
My dear Jennie surprised me with a new wine bengaline reception dress that she made for me. Didn't want to trust it to anyone else. It is beautiful. She also brought the bride's second-day dress for me to see. It is a Prussian blue wool challis.

ry Megan in Corset Cover and Petticoat

Mary Megan's Silk Wedding Dress

Mary Megan's Second-day Dress and Trimmed Hat

December 24, 1890—I feel content with the outcome of my handiwork on the wedding dress. It is of white silk de chine with a ruffle-trimmed yoke of satin ribbon lattice-work highlighted with filling stitches and pearls. It was my own idea, and I must say, it suits Mary Megan—dainty but with quality. I've been working on it for 2 months.

December 25, 1890—Another Christmas and another wedding, a truly happy event. Mary Megan is now married to Thomas Benjamin Savage, the grandson of Matthew's old commanding officer. They will soon be moving out onto the caprock. It is called the Llano Estacado, which means "Staked Plains." It sounds rather wild and unsettled, but Mary Megan says she feels a glory in getting to be a real pioneer and welcomes the challenge.

I have had a good and blessed life. Now I can help Mary Megan start her new home. She will be needing a lot of linens and quilts. My thrill of settling a new frontier will be carried on by Mary Megan, who has promised to send me frequent letters. Perhaps one day she will continue the family story in her own journal.